To Anne Kelsey with love

Blake Johnson

March 25, 1986

Bird Magic

Purple Finches

Bird Magic

by Blake Johnson

with photographs by the author

Blake Johnson, Publisher
Englewood, Florida

Arcade Lithographing Corporation

Blake Johnson
24 Oakwood Drive, North
Englewood, FL 33533

Printed in the United States of America

*To my wife, Margaret,
whose constant support and
help made this book possible.*

Table of Contents

5 Dedication

7 Table of Contents

9 Acknowledgments

11 Introduction Oliver H. Hewitt, PhD.

13 A New Approach to Bird Photography

17 Black-capped Chickadee

24 American Goldfinch

28 Red Crossbill

32 Purple Finch

36 Pine Siskin

40 Evening Grosbeak

46 Gray Catbird

50 Robin

60 Loon

61 Eastern Phoebe

64 Tree Swallow

68 Cedar Waxwing

72 Wood Thrush

78 Ruby-throated Hummingbird, Albino

82 Bullock's Oriole

86 Northern Flicker

90 Great Blue Heron New Hampshire

94 Wood Duck

96 Donaldson's Stereo Strobe Camera

97 Great Horned Owl

98 Saw-whet Owl

100 Snowy Owl

102 Burrowing Owl

104 Little Blue Heron

106 Wood Stork

110 Sandhill Crane

112 Black Skimmer

114 Roseate Spoonbill

118 Laughing Gull

122 Great Blue Heron Florida

126 Epilogue David L. Thomas, MD

Acknowledgments

I do not think that I ever would have started making pictures of birds if it had not been for Dr. Harold Edgerton, who adapted his stroboscopic systems for the use of nature photographers.

I am particularly grateful to the staffs of the Massachusetts and the National Audubon Societies of the 1950s. Their interest in and the promotion of my work gave me the confidence to continue my endeavors.

I also thank family, other relatives and friends who became enthusiastic about what I was trying to do. They helped in many ways such as finding interesting situations to photograph and promoting lecture dates.

I also appreciate the advice Dr. Oliver Hewitt gave me after we settled in Florida.

To Skip Pape who helped me in mastering my IBM Personal Computer and its "Writing Assistant" disk which I used constantly in creating this book.

I am grateful for the cover designed by Don Kent.

I wish to thank Dr. David L. Thomas for the Epilogue.

Introduction

George Blake Johnson is an inventive pioneer in photography of birds and especially in the use of stroboscopic techniques to portray birds in full flight. He has succeeded in producing photographs in sharp focus showing action in great detail.

This beautiful volume is partly autobiographical. Blake Johnson explains how he was led into bird photography by his bird-watching wife and children; how he used a stroboscopic invention of Dr. Harold Edgerton of the Massachusetts Institute of Technology in Cambridge, Massachusetts; and by dint of much experimentation, how he worked out his techniques with great success.

We can enjoy the results of his work with photographs of thirty species of birds taken in New England and Florida; and for each species, his personal and sometimes whimsical account of his experiences.

Blake Johnson's photographs have been published in journals of natural history, photography and ornithology. I am glad that he has brought them together in one volume.

A bird photographer becomes intimate with his subjects. Blake Johnson's accounts of his adventures are personal and full of delight.

Oliver H. Hewitt, Ph.D.
Charlotte Harbor, Florida
March 1985

A New Approach to Bird Photography

As World War II was drawing toward a final confrontation, I was still commanding officer of the *USS Kern*, AOG-2. The Kern was an auxiliary gasoline tanker. Her mission was to keep the tanks full on the new partially secured air strips in the Marianas and the Carolines in the western Pacific. While we were in the middle of this assignment, orders came through for me to go to Seattle and report for duty as executive officer on the *USS Bexar*, APA-237.

The *Bexar* was a large attack transport vessel designed to carry our forces and their equipment to the shores of the enemy's homeland. A week before the ship was due to be commissioned, thanks to President Truman, the war came to a sudden end—a tragic one for the enemy. However, it saved no one knows how many thousands and thousands of lives on both sides. I could have remained with the ship for a shake-down cruise to Pearl Harbor, but I opted for out.

On my way home I realized that I would not find things the same as when I left. After all, I had been absent for almost three years. When I finally arrived at my home in Framingham Center, Massachusetts, I was greeted with great excitement and enthusiasm. It took some time for the expressions of welcome home and love to subside. When they did I noted that both my son and my daughter had grown in stature and seemed more mature than I had anticipated. My wife was serene and seemed to be in command of the situation.

After we began to get used to being a family of four again, I found that their interests had changed. The conversation at meals seemed to be mostly about birds. It was not long before I realized that they had become ardent bird watchers. This was a bit different from what I was watching out for from the bridge of my ship. It seemed like rather a dull pastime.

I had already pretty well rid myself of calling the kitchen "the galley," the wall "the bulkhead" and the floor "the deck," but my family continued talking about redstarts, white-eyed vireos and rufous-sided towhees ad infinitum. I decided that I could not infringe on their pursuits. They were too dedicated to them. However, I could join them—join them by trying to photograph the birds they were watching. But I did not want to photograph birds perching on a limb. I wanted to freeze their images in full flight.

WWII camouflage sheets make a blind.

I had heard of Dr. Harold Edgerton's development of the strobe lamp. I found that the lamps were being made by the Dormitzer Co. of Cambridge. It did not take me long to acquire two lamps and two Synctron Power Packs to energize the lamps.

Now to arrange a set-up where I could have a chance of obtaining some flight pictures. I moved our feeder to a place outside the kitchen window. I devised a blind in front of the feeder, set my Leica on its tripod in it and focused it on the center of the feeder. The lamps were fastened to brackets on the outside wall. I used a DeGoff air cable release to activate the shutter and the lamps. A long tube went through the kitchen window with the bulb hanging over the sink. I do not think that my wife was very happy with this arrangement. However, she was a very good sport about it.

I used to sit at the breakfast table and, whenever I saw some activity, get up and rush to my bulb. Of course, after every exposure I had to go out and advance the film. I obtained a quantity of good shots of birds on the feeder but as far as flight was concerned it was a failure. The closest I ever came was the head of the bird just coming in to the frame or the tail feathers going out.

The human reaction was just not fast enough to anticipate a bird's position and catch it in the center of the field. There had to be an electronic way for the bird to take its own picture when passing through a predetermined spot. The logical method would be to have a beam of light with a photoelectric cell connected to a solenoid on the camera. This posed many problems. The Photo Switch Company of Cambridge helped me to work out a tripping device which could be used on my feeding station. Later the apparatus was modified so that it could be used in the field.

I soon realized that the electronic flash developed by Dr. Harold Edgerton was a revolution in the photography of fast-moving objects. It had already won its spurs in solving problems in World War II. Now in the early 1950s it had been made available to camera enthusiasts such as myself. Before, making close-up photos of small birds in flight resulted in nothing but a blurred image. Now birds' acrobatics in mid-air could be recorded factually.

I desired to have everything available to make my efforts successful. I therefore purchased booster units to become a part of my Synctron power-packs.

Without the photo tripping device I had added to my equipment and regardless of the intensity of the lamps, I could not react fast enough to catch the bird in the field of view of my lens. Birds only four to six feet away, flying at fifteen miles per hour, would be in range for only one-tenth of a second, faster birds even less.

Chickadee making a landing.

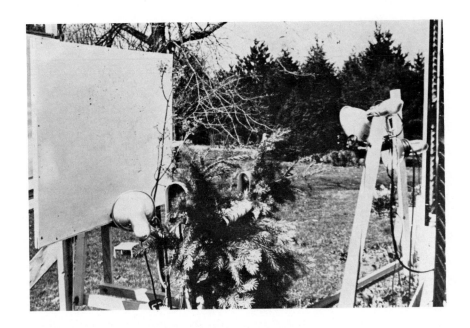

For contrast to the stroboscopic photographs, I am adding a few pictures I made after we moved to the southwest coast of Florida.

To get back to the use of strobe flash again: Pictures may be made in bright sunshine, with the sun covered by heavy clouds, or even at night. The f-stop of the camera is set at its smallest opening. The exposure was controlled by the distance of the lamps from the subject—four to six feet. Unless one had an artificial background with strobe lamps focused on it, everything else, except the subject, would be black. As fas as I was concerned, this was just plain theory. If it truly worked, to me it would be just plain magic.

I set up again to try to obtain pictures of birds in flight, this time in front of a window in the sun porch of our home in Framingham Center, Massachusetts. This looked out on a 150-foot spread of lawn, bordered by an old stone wall. On the other side of the wall was a stand of second-growth hardwood. This made an excellent jumping-off place for birds to fly to the feeder.

I first had to design a stand to accommodate my photo switch and the feeder. The photo switch came in three parts: the light source, the sensor and the controller. The controller adjusted the sensitivity of the switch to the speed of the object passing through its beam. It was contained in a metal box about 8″x10″x4″ with a long cord. I made the stand from various lengths of 3/4-inch galvanized pipe with elbows, Ts and other fittings. When completed it was on a nine-foot length of pipe. This could be thrust in the ground at a correct distance from the lens of the camera in the sun porch.

Next I had to have a background lighted by two strobe lamps just as objects passing through the beam were to be illuminated. If I did not do this, the pictures would appear to have been taken by flash in the dark of night. The background had to be illuminated by strobe, otherwise shadows would show up. The two lamps on either side of the window where the camera lens was were directed on the beam light. The ones for the background were placed a little below and in back of the feeding tray. They were all plugged into Synctron Power Packs.

Inside the sun porch I had the choice of using my Leica, my Hasselblad or my three-by-four Linhof. The f-stop was set at its smallest opening. The exposure was determined by the distance of the lamps from the subject. The beauty of this was that daylight had no effect on the results. I could operate the set-up in bright sunlight, on cloudy days or in semi-darkness. The wiring of this was a little complicated, but it could be hooked up to AC or dry cell batteries.

Often, as it appears in the photo above, the feeding tray was arranged with various varieties of branches. This was to provide a more or less natural setting for the birds.

Now I was ready to put to the test this modern (modern I guess for those days of the 1950s) "Rube Goldberg" contraption of electronic and photographic components. It was weird that in order to make this arrangement perform one had to be something of a plumber, carpenter and electrician, to say nothing of being sort of a camera bug. I am sure that the Chickadee, the first bird to bring this inanimate apparatus to life, cared little about making history. Massachusetts, I believe, claims the Black-capped Chickadee as its state bird. However, it gives a great many people pleasure watching it go to and from the feeding tray with a sunflower seed in its bill. In normal horizontal flight, this bird has a wingbeat of about eight flaps per second and travels up to a speed of from 25 and 30 miles per hour.

The Chickadee is purported to be a very resourceful bird. It is known to carry off its sunflower seeds and other bits of food and to conceal them for future consumption.

When consuming its meal on the site, it will fly off the feeding tray with a large sunflower seed in its bill to a nearby tree. Then it will hold the seed with its claws against the branch and pick the seed open with its bill to obtain the contents. In winter, when satisfied, they will descend to a snowbank and quench their thirst by swallowing small pieces. They are very hardy and warmly clad in light and very downy feathers which protect them from the icy blasts of the season.

18. Chickadee dropping from skies.
19. Flaps down ready to land.

19

Chickadee at rest.

21. *Chickadee springs up with sunflower seed.*
22, 23. *Chickadees chasing each other around the feeder is one of the many exhibitions these birds put on.*

The feeder is not always the most peaceful place for birds. Here, two Goldfinches in competition for seeds confront each other. Then, as if blasted off by Mission Control, they rise aloft, beak to beak, until they disappear out of range of the camera. The Goldfinch is an active and conspicuous little bird with its black wings and gold body undulating over field and garden. It is sometimes referred to as the wild canary due to its resemblance to the domesticated bird.

Goldfinches are partial to gardens and the surroundings of homes in a suburban area. As summer wanes they go to the fields where there is an ample supply of weeds. They can be seen climbing the stalk of a tall slender plant until it arches over like the end of a rainbow. They then are observed hanging and moving about, head downwards, while cracking open and consuming the seeds. As colder weather arrives many disappear, headed for warmer climes. Others remain. However, the male loses its brilliant colors and more nearly resembles its mate.

25. *Two male Goldfinches blasting up.*
26, 27. *The Goldfinches shout at each other.*

One morning, as I was getting dressed, looking out of our bedroom window, I saw a flight of Crossbills preparing to make a landing in the trees on the other side of our stone wall. I yelled down to the kitchen, "Set thirty-three more places for breakfast—the Crossbills are dropping in." Our son and daughter, who were just about ready to take off for school, knew what this meant. My wife automatically put my morning meal on hold until after I had taken a few shots of the newcomers.

The Crossbills migrate from an extremely frigid northern Canada to a less cold and less snowy Massachusetts.

The male bird in winter is of a brick red color. The female is sort of a grayish to yellowish olive, with blackish wings and tail. Their bills do cross. This, I gather, is to make it easier for them to split open the pine cone seeds which make up a good part of their diet.

View out the window.

29. A Crossbill taking off with a
sunflower seed.
30, 31. Crossbills at the feeder.

The Purple Finch is a year-around resident of the area. It does not give way easily its place on the feeder to other birds arriving from northern climes.

The male of that species is crimson or purplish crimson that is deepest around the head. The female is pale brown, streaked with darker brown.

Early records, according to Nuttall (1830) say great flocks could be seen roving around the countryside. Apparently, at this time birds such as these were trapped or netted to put in cages for sale. The Purple Finch had a song to match the most melodious Canary. To quote Nuttall directly, "The males are very bold and pugnacious in confinement, attempting to destroy every other bird introduced into the same cage. They also bite severely when taken up wounded, but are directly reconciled to the cage, finding their most important wants so amply supplied."

Today this seems very cruel and unforgiving just to have a singing bird hanging in a cage in one's parlor. I remember as a boy some seventy years ago having a Canary brought into my sickroom and feeling the same way. When spring came I opened the window and the door of the cage and let the little bird fly out into freedom. I did not realize that this was the cruelest thing I could do.

You can see from the photos with the strobe light that I caught the birds in their own environment, and they were free to go without being any worse for their capture on film.

33. *Male Purple Finch about to land. Female looks up.*
34. *Two Purple Finches on a collision course.*
35. *The females confront each other.*

33

34

The winter of 1953 must have been very harsh up north because all kinds of birds seemed to be descending in great flocks to the feeders in our vicinity. My feeder was no exception. As a matter of fact, on account of our location we had a greater number of birds than anyone else around us. Pine Siskins and Evening Grosbeaks came in masses of fifty or sixty each. The competition between these two species was horrendous.

On waking up in the morning I would go to the window to look down at my feeder. More often than not it was empty. Then I would look at the elm slightly to the rear and to the right of my feeder. On its branches there could be twenty or more Siskins waiting for the feeder to be replenished. Before I could get back into the house, the Siskins had swarmed down to the feeder and perched on any convenient piece of my equipment they could find.

Then, as I went upstairs to my room to look out the window, I would see the Grosbeaks leaving their roosts on the trees behind the stone wall and flying to the feeding area.

The Siskin is similar to a Goldfinch in size but a little slimmer. It is streaked grayish-brown with some white and a tinge of yellow. They were continually squabbling among themselves as well as with other birds larger than they. They would not hesitate to challenge a Crossbill or even the larger Grosbeak.

Pine Siskin composite.

37

Pine Siskin challenging Evening Grosbeak.

39. Two Siskins cavorting mid-air.

The Evening Grosbeak was first noted in the central part of the United States during the 1850s. Around the turn of the century it started migrating eastwards. By the time these pictures were made, they were winter visitors to almost every town in Massachusetts and Rhode Island. Their presence comes with a miraculous suddenness. Some day in November or December there will be none. The next morning you will see ten to thirty hovering over the feeder.

The Evening Grosbeak is eight and one-half inches long. The Pine Siskin that already dominates the feeder is only a little over five inches. It would appear that there might be confrontations between these two. The male is a very striking and aristocratic-looking bird. It has a black head with golden forehead and black wings with inner wing feathers of white. The tail feathers are black. The female has a darkish grey head and a lighter grey body. The wings are similar to those of the male.

The Grosbeaks are fascinating to watch. Sometimes there will be as many as eight on the feeder at the same time. Then for some unknown reason they will all take off together. Seeds will fly as their feet push them into the air with their wings beating at a frequency of about fifty-five strokes per second. Then in a wink they will be out of range and other birds will swoop in to take their place. The mystery is which bird gives the signal for the sudden departure.

41. Evening Grosbeak takes off over Pine Siskin.
42. Evening Grosbeaks and Pine Siskins.
43. A lift-off.
44, 45. Female Evening Grosbeaks.

41

43

The Catbird usually arrives in the Framingham area early in May. They settle around our house and garden as if they had returned to their real home. The bird hops from branch to branch in the shrubbery and then to the garden and back on to the lawn. While doing this it makes a "mewing" sound similar to that of a cat. Hence the name.

The Catbird is known as the great imitator. It is not only the sounds of the cat they mimic. They can create the songs of other birds. When courtship commences they strut about, chase each other in flight, and there is a great outpouring of song. Nuptials over, they both set to work building their nest. Song and sounds, as is true with other birds, then cease. This is done, of course, to prevent disclosure of the location of their nest.

In this case, the nest was built right up against the blank wall of our garage in thick shrubbery. I had to wait until the birds were hatched before setting up my equipment. When they emerged from their eggs, I studied the flight route the parents made to and from the nest as they brought worms and insects to the gaping mouths of their young. Even so, it was very difficult to place my photo-switch in the path of flight.

The Catbird is of slate color to light grey. The tail is black and rounded. It is a little smaller than a robin. Its range is from northern Canada to Central America. It stops off during the winter in Florida.

Catbird about to feed fledglings.

47

Catbird approaching nest.

48

Catbird leaving nest.

49

Spring and the Robins arrive.

As winter relaxed its grip on New England and spring gradually approached, I began to think of dismantling my feeder set-up. I would have to do it anyway before the mowing season started, and this was only a matter of days away.

What to do next? When the first Robin descended on our lawn and cocked its head to one side, as if to listen to or eyeball a worm, an idea started formulating in my mind. Would it be possible to move my equipment into a nesting site? Of course, it would be possible, but could it be done in such a way so as not to disturb the bird and possibly force it to abandon its nest? This required some thought and planning.

When a pair of Robins had completed their nest and the mother bird laid its eggs and started sitting on them, I decided to put up a strobe lamp with its power pack directly in front of the nest. This I was able to do during the short period the bird was away. When the Robin returned and saw this strange object on its front door step, it circled around and alighted on a nearby branch. It seemed not to take it long to decide that what I placed there did not offer any threat to its home. It then hopped directly to the nest and settled down in it. Then it was no problem to move my camera on its tripod into position and make some pictures.

The next step was to wait until the birds were hatched. When this occurred I started to study the paths of flight the birds took as they landed

50

on the nest to feed their young and to note in what direction they took off in quest of more grubs and worms. I wanted to place my photo switch just about where I thought they would land. This was a tricky task, because the birds were not long away from their nest and there were a few branches which had to be cut off in order to obtain a clear line of sight.

When this was all done I set what I thought was the correct f-stop and let the birds take their own pictures. I should mention here that the 1/5,000-second flash has no effect on the action of the birds. When I thought I had taken a sufficient number of exposures, I took the film down to my darkroom and developed it. I could then judge whatever changes in my settings would be advisable for future pictures.

One thing I did not have to worry about was the weather. Whether there was bright sunlight or heavy clouds and shadows made no difference. No matter how familiar Robins are, these photos yield real close-up views and produce details of the bird itself which can only be found by examining the skins. They also help in a study of the bird's family life.

When the cold weather comes, the Robins start southward. One January, hundreds of them soared over our home in southwest Florida. A few found our pyrocantha vine on the rear of our garage. It was not long before they stripped it of all its red berries. Soon they were staggering drunkenly on our concrete drive and in the process were coughing up purplish-red sputum. These stains were very difficult to eradicate. The Robins were with us only a few days before continuing on their migration.

Robins eating pyracantha berries in Florida.

Robin alighting with a beakload of insects.

54. *Robin offering worms.*
55. *Robin shoving worms down fledgling's throat. Note partly closed eyelid on small bird.*

Up to this time, all my photos were made from subjects around our home. After I had removed the equipment from outside the window of our sun porch, I had set up in only two different locations. These were for the Robin and the Catbird. I now wanted to discover whether I could find photographic subjects around our camp on Squam Lake, New Hampshire. I was sure that I would have to do considerable improvising over what I had been doing.

After we had arrived and got unloaded and pretty well settled in our cottage, I started cruising the vicinity to see what I could find. I thought I saw some activity in a tall hemlock right on the shore of the lake, but it was becoming too dark to see what it was. I would have to wait until morning.

The first thing the next day, I launched our canoe and went to the hemlock I was looking at the evening before. Sure enough, half way up and well into the tree was a Robin feeding her young in a nest. This was a challenge! I remember seeing a long ladder alongside our neighbor's boathouse. I summoned help and we waded in the lake to the tree. With the bottom of the ladder in about two feet of water, we eased the top down to rest just below the nest. This, of course, was done while the parent bird was off hunting for worms and bugs. When the Robin returned it did not seem to be in the least disturbed by what it found leaning against its tree. While waiting and watching, two Loons surfaced to see what was going on.

When I felt that the birds had become accustomed to the new object at their front door, I climbed the ladder and hung the power pack and battery from one side of the ladder. The lamp and the camera on its tripod I clamped to the tops of the two ends of the ladder. With all connections made, I brought the tripping cord down and hung the push button on a rung three feet above the surface. I was all set for action. I tried to catch the bird as it flew on or off the nest, but I was not quick enough. Each time the Robin approached suddenly from different areas. I did, however, obtain some feeding scenes.

This tree was adjacent to the property of my niece and her husband. Some twenty years later it was where *ON GOLDEN POND* was filmed. I wonder what Henry Fonda and Kathryn Hepburn, playing the parts of Norman and Ethel Thayer, would have thought having this oddity in their view.

56. Feeding completed. Robin flies off to gather more food.

58. Robin in hemlock feeding young. Insert: Photo set-up.

59. Robin putting a bit of worm in closing beak.

Two Loons on Squam Lake, New Hampshire.

Out of the nest almost ready to fly.

On the other side of the boathouse from which I took the ladder for my hemlock scene, there was a Phoebe's nest. It was tucked in right under the eaves. This was a very difficult place to photograph with my strobe lamps, but I decided to give it a try.

The Robin and Phoebe locations were excellent for me because our camp adjoined the land where these two birds chose to build their nests. This meant that I had plenty of volunteer help in the setting up and taking down of my equipment. I really appreciated this, especially when later I went to places far from home base.

There were four little birds in the nest. The parents were constantly coming and going. A couple of rainy days gave me the chance to work out a solution to the problem of how I was going to make pictures without driving the birds from their home.

When I first started to set up my equipment, I was unmercifully dive-bombed by the two parents. I stood my ground without moving a muscle. It was only a matter of moments before they ceased these actions and went back to the business of feeding their young. Apparently, I was accepted, and I went on with what I had begun.

Though Phoebes prefer to build their nest on some kind of a shelf or small protrusion, this nest was plastered to the wall of the building. Each baby bird consumes half its weight a day in bugs. Among the many pests that these birds—adults and young—eat are mosquitoes, gypsy moths and other destructive moths. They catch these insects in full flight. Both parents take part in the feeding. One always remains on the nest to drive off predators.

The Phoebe has a wing spread of eleven inches, compared to a Siskin's nine inches. In color it is chiefly greyish olive, paling somewhat toward the tail. All in all, it is a rounder, more puffed-up bird than the sleeker Siskin.

62. The parent thrusts its bill into the wide open mouth of the bird in the corner.

63. The Phoebe flies up to the nest with a beak full of food. From observing many similar nesting activities, it seems to me that the most audacious and vociferous of the fledglings gets fed first and the less aggressive last. Notice the sad little bird with its mouth shut. Is it going to survive? Survival of the fittest would seem to apply.

The Tree Swallow is the first of the birds to arrive in the North and the last to depart for the South. This is because they can exist on berries and are not dependent on insects for their sustenance.

My wife's mother, Mrs. Arthur Ingraham, had her home in Little Compton, Rhode Island. She was an ardent bird enthusiast and was interested in my photographic efforts. On one of our many visits to her place, she pointed out the nesting site of a pair of Tree Swallows. As time went on, through friends and neighbors, she found other locations for me to consider.

While in earlier days Tree Swallows nested in hollow trees or abandoned holes of Woodpeckers, now they mostly use bird-houses, nesting boxes or crevices in buildings. This pair had a flower pot sealed at the open end, with an enlarged drainage hole for the entrance. It was hung in a grape arbor. The people who placed it there could not foresee the difficulties they caused me in setting up my equipment. It took me some three and one-half days before I could make the first exposure. This time I had taken a developing kit so that at the end of the day I could see what improvements I could make in the position of my camera and in the f-stop I had used.

With the fledglings grown and departed from the nest, the family remained in the area until the really cold weather signaled them to start south. They followed the coastline and stopped off from place to place to eat berries and to receive additional hundreds to their flock.

We had a winter home in Cape Haze on the southwest coast of Florida. When the Tree Swallows arrived, their numbers could be estimated only in the thousands. They would swoop around the area and descend in a swarm on a wax myrtle tree to eat the berries. When the tree was stripped of fruit they would shoot up in what looked like a great puff of black smoke from an explosion and drop down to the next tree. After cleaning the area of everything suitable to their diet, they disappeared as suddenly as they arrived.

65. *(Top) The Tree Swallow is about to alight on the flower pot. Notice the large white cardboard in the rear. This is so that I would not have a totally black background.*

65. *(Bottom) The Tree Swallow is leaving the nest, tripping the shutter on its way for more food.*

66. *Tree Swallow approaches nest and young scream for food.*

Tree Swallows swarm down on wax myrtle bushes in Florida.

On another visit to Little Compton, Mrs. Ingraham told me of a new nesting site in which I might be interested. She had already obtained the approval of the owner of the property on which the nest was located for me to come and go as I pleased.

The nest turned out to be that of a pair of Cedar Waxwings. It was half way up a heavily foliated maple tree. The tree was separated from the road to Sakonnet Point by a stone wall. The nest was well in toward the trunk of the tree. The birds were already feeding the chicks with black cherries. I was most anxious to get shots of the birds as they flew on and off the nest in the process of feeding their young. It posed a real problem deciding how to do this without frightening the birds to the extent that they might abandon the nest. Fortunately, our son was on this visit with us and he helped resolve the dilemma.

We finally went to a local painter and obtained from him a combination ladder. It consisted of two ladders that spread out in the form of an A. Another ladder went up through the vertex of the A and could be locked in at any desired height. We were able to place this central ladder so that its top was on the same level as the nest. This accomplished, we called it a day. We wanted the birds to become used to having this strange object right in front of them.

We returned the next morning with a long two-by-six plank. This we ran over one of the rungs of the ladder to a lower branch of the tree. This gave me a platform of sorts on which to stand to make adjustments to the equipment. The camera, two strobe lamps with their power packs and a battery were either clamped or hung to the upper part of the ladder. As my son watched me on the ladder, he remarked that he had not progressed far enough in Medical School to treat broken bones.

The controller was placed on a step ladder on the ground. I covered it with a World War II rubberized camouflage sheet when not in use. The most difficult operation was to get the photo-electric tripping unit in place where the birds would pass through it as they flew up to and away from the nest. All the electrical connections then had to be made, being sure that we had the power packs turned off before leaving. Now, as I had brought down to ground level a wire with a push button, I could let the birds take their own pictures, or I could do it manually.

The illustration opposite shows most of the elements that I used to make pictures of the Cedar Waxwing. On the step ladder is the controller which allowed me to adjust the sensitivity of the sensor. The two Synctron power packs which energize the strobe lamps are hanging from either side of the ladder.

One of the Cedar Waxwings feeding the young. Note berry almost down the throat of bird on left.

The Cedar Waxwings were most cooperative. The birds derived their names from the fact that one or two of their feathers were tipped with a spot resembling red sealing wax. They choose New England as one of their breeding areas. They can be seen in Florida in the winter, stretched out, perching on a high wire looking like a long string of beads.

71. *Cedar Waxwing, leaving the nest in search of more food, passes through the beam and registers its image on film.*

Another nest had been located for me in Little Compton. This time it was that of a Wood Thrush. It was a bit unusual because the bird had picked up a piece of cloth to use for the foundation of its structure. The nest was about twenty feet high. I used two trestle ladders with two planks across them—one to sit on, the other to stand on. I used the latter to arrange my apparatus and to focus the camera, which was a three-by-four Linhof. I chose to take pictures of nesting scenes before moving in my photo switch tripping components.

The illustration shows me sitting on the bottom plank ready to push the button when I saw an interesting pose. The push button was, of course, connected to the solenoid on the camera, which activated the shutter and strobe lamps. Notice the battery on the far side, which gives the power to the Synctron units that activate the lamps. The 1/5000-second time of the flash does not bother the birds in the least. As a matter of fact, if my eyes blinked at the right time, I would have no way of knowing whether the lamps flashed or not.

After placing the photo-switch, which was mounted on a long pipe, I clamped a newly acquired stereo camera alongside the Linhof. It was wired so the two cameras would operate simultaneously. I then stepped aside and let the birds take over, photographing themselves as they flew on and off the nest.

The Wood Thrush arrives in New England during the middle of May. It announces its presence with melodious song. Its tones seem to harmonize with whatever area it is in—woods, gardens or fields. When nest building starts, all song ceases until the young are old enough to go off on their own. This is so as not to give away to predators the location of the nest.

Friends and passers-by were attracted by the view of my set-ups and came to see what was going on. However, they never came close enough to disturb the subjects.

I never became weary of observing the development of the young and watching the coming and going of the parents. Many times, this meant no lunch or supper. Fortunately, my family was understanding and forgiving.

73. *Set-up at the Wood Thrush nesting site.*
74, 75. *The Wood Thrush and three little
ones. Note that the largest one in
the middle appears to have the first choice.*
76, 77. *The Wood Thrush glides down
from its nest in the lilac bush, and
flies off to gather more sustenance.*

One day in the summer of 1953, Russell Mason of the Massachusetts Audubon Society called me to say that there was a Ruby-throated Hummingbird in Gardiner, Maine, and asked if I would go there and take some pictures of this very rare bird.

Fortunately, I had my son, who could help me in my photographic endeavors. We wasted no time in packing up and heading "Down East." The bird was frequenting the home of a Miss Bates. When we arrived, we found that the Hummer was coming to a feeder made of a pill bottle painted red, filled with a solution of sugar and water, to a wire outside Miss Bates' study window. We could not believe our eyes when we first saw the bird. It was snow white, and it looked like a ballet dancer as it was rapidly approaching its nectar. It would alight on a tiger lily in the garden a short distance from the study. If there were any other Hummingbirds inthe vicinity, as oftentimes there were, the Albino would drive them off before taking its fill at Miss Bates' feeder.

Miss Bates' farm and garden.

Hummingbird flying to feeder.

Hummingbird at feeder.

Hummingbird on lily.

After taking several black and white as well as color photographs at the feeder I, after some urging, persuaded Miss Bates to let me move the nectar bottle to the tiger lily. I did this in the hopes of capturing the bird in more natural surroundings. On its first trip back it went directly to the window and seemed to express dismay at the removal of its dinner. It flew up and down the window and around the house, finally darting off into space.

We feared that the bird would never come back. We were not reassured by Miss Bates' remarking that the feeder had never been moved. We waited for more than two hours, trying to mollify Miss Bates. Just as we were about to leave in despair, the Hummer came out of the blue, darting around the landscape. We watched it breathlessly. Suddenly it zoomed down onto the lily and partook of the bottle. As soon as it had its fill and flew off, we immediately returned the feeder to its regular place. It grew late in the day, but we were agreed in not leaving until it returned to the window.

It seemed ages before it did return. But only then was our mission accomplished. We thanked Miss Bates for her patience and understanding and then packed up and started our long drive home.

Hummingbird arrives at feeder.

81

One day in March of 1953, I went to Audubon House in Boston to show Russell Mason, the executive director, some of my latest stroboscopic photographs of wintering Finches. Before I left, he asked me if I would consider going to Falmouth for two or three days to take pictures of a bird whose identity had been puzzling birders and ornithologists for days. I agreed to start out the next morning for the home of a Mr. Collins in Plymouth, Massachusetts.

This particular year there had been a record number of Orioles reported. There was one that kept coming to the feeder that seemed different from the Baltimore Orioles which were common to the area. The thought was that this might be a bird from the west known as a Bullock's Oriole. It was hoped that my high-speed photographs would settle the argument.

The bird was a regular visitor. It fed from a mixture of suet and seed in half of a coconut shell. As mentioned before, my light source and sensor were mounted on long sections of 3/4-inch pipe. I generally could thrust them into the ground, but sometimes I had to use a crowbar. This time neither way would work because it was necessary to set up my things on a broad stone terrace. I became really frustrated. The Collins were as upset as I was and were very sympathetic.

Set-up at Collins' house, Falmouth, Massachusetts.

I wandered around the house and finally took a long look at the clothes reel. That was it. I went to the front of the house and found Mr. Collins glumly looking around, and I asked him if we could not take the reel off its pole, invert it, and use it as a quadrupod. He was very enthusiastic about the idea. However, first we would have to ask Mrs. Collins to take down the laundry drying on it. This she was most happy to do.

It remained only for Mr. Collins to put a pipe in the ground on which to fasten my background. I hasten to mention again that this was necessary because I had to illuminate the background with strobe lamps in order not to have my subjects look as if they had been shot in the black of night. After two days there, I felt I had plenty of exposures to satisfy the purpose of my mission.

The photographs turned out far better than my expectations. I took them right in to Audubon House. They were shown to many people, including Ludlow Griscom of the Museum of Comparative Zoology at Harvard. He felt the pictures showed that the male bird at least was a Bullock's, and he suggested that duplicates be sent to George M. Sutton, professor of zoology and curator of birds at the University of Oklahoma. He sent a long reply which proved that the two birds in the Collins yard were "Bullocki," although records showed that they very rarely strayed so far east.

Bullock's Oriole and Pine Siskin on coconut shell filled with suet and seeds.
84, 85. Bullock's Oriole flying off. Notice black streak under throat.

Another call came from Mrs. Ingraham saying that a pair of birds were working on a nesting place on her property. I packed up all my paraphernalia. My wife and I started off again for Little Compton. This time we found a pair of Flickers that had been driven off by Starlings from the nesting hole they had started high up on a telephone pole.

The Flickers then started on a box which covered an artesian well. Mrs. Ingraham's handyman had noticed wood chips outside the box which they were trying to bore through. The box was made of three-quarter-inch boards. The next morning the hole looked as if it had been completed, and there were no longer any signs of wood chips. This was not surprising because Flickers are known to work the clock around, and when completed they pick up all the evidence of their operations and put them back in the nest. This was all done two weeks before we arrived on the scene.

Once more I had to work out the same problem of getting my apparatus placed. This time it was more difficult because the site was right out on an open field. The illustration shows on the far left the tripod for the camera, four strobe lamps focused on the front of the box and the light source of the sensor directly in front. The lamp on the far right was to give a little illumination to the background. These units could be covered and left out overnight. When I was ready to make pictures I had to bring in and connect up the battery, power packs and camera. The photographs tell the rest of the story.

Flickers at nesting site. Male perched on top, female flying off.

Flicker approaching nest.

Flicker about to depart.

Flicker flying off. See the yellow under the wing. This is why it is sometimes called the
Yellow-shafted Flicker.

Cove in Squam Lake New Hampshire.

Across the lake from our camp where I photographed the Robin and Phoebe there is a deep cove. Going by it one day, I noticed three Great Blue Herons flying around the top of a tall beech tree. I decided to try out my new long lens.

The lake was quite low for this season of the year. I knew the only way to get anywhere near the tree was by canoe. This was not a very good platform to take a picture from, especially if you had to make an exposure under 1/125th of a second. For me this would be a different challenge from using the strobe.

91. Great Blue Heron alighting.

90

It was a wonderfully peaceful spot. As this shore was inaccessible by land, it was completely wild. The water was like glass. There were grasses breaking through the surface, and the area was spotted with small hummocks of land crowned with wild azalea bushes in full bloom. In paddling toward the base of the beech I had to circumvent one of those hummocks in order not to disturb a Loon that was nesting on it. When I reached a spot where I had the clearest view of the Herons, I lowered over the side a rope with a stone attached to it to hold me in place. Then I started making the pictures of the three Herons.

Although I could not actually make it out, there appeared to be a nest and a pair of Herons were trying to drive an intruder off. The Herons arrive early in the spring and leave before the end of summer. When I was doing this work (I should not say work because for me it was a sport), I did not realize that some thirty years later I would be photographing this same breed of Heron high up in pine trees around our home in Florida.

92. Great Blue Herons around nest,
     apparently driving off an intruder.

93. Heron looking down to nest.

93

Nuttall, who in the early nineteenth century ranked with Wilson and Audubon as an outstanding ornithologist, said in 1833 that the Wood Duck was the most beautiful of ducks.

Forbush, 100 years later, extolled the exquisiteness of its colors and shimmering feathers even more strongly. He also stated that the Wood Duck, in the first ten years of the twentieth century, was headed for the same fate as that of the Passenger Pigeon. In 1850 it was estimated that there were over one billion Passenger Pigeons in the United States. They were so tame that they were killed by the thousands and shipped to markets in large cities, where they ended up as whole squabs on the dinner table. I can remember that around 1910, whole squabs on toast was one of my favorite dishes. In the 1920s there was not a Passenger Pigeon left. They had become extinct.

It seemed to many that the Wood Duck was headed for the same fate. It was the favorite of duck hunters, who banged away at it unmercifully. The feathers were used in the millinery trade. They also were made up into wonderful flies for the trout fisherman. They were even stuffed and mounted by taxidermists and sold to grace the shelves of living rooms. Wood Ducks became so scarce that they began to be imported from Belgium at exhorbitant prices. The Belgians realized the value of the bird. They were able to domesticate them and raise them for sale.

Finally, state and federal laws were enacted protecting the bird at all times. This all happened over sixty years ago. We can thank the environmentalists of the time for stepping in so that the Wood Duck is a viable part of our wildlife scene today.

I can do no better than quote a sentence from Forbush: "Loveliest of all waterfowl, the Wood Duck stands supreme. Deep flooded swamps where ancient mossy trees overhang the dark still waters, secluded pools amid the scattered pines where water-lilies lift their snowy heads and turtles bask in the sun, purling brooks flowing through dense woodlands where light and shade fleck the splashing waters, slow-flowing creeks and marshy ponds— these are the haunts of the Wood Duck."

I did not have to hunt out any of these places. Just as the leaves were beginning to turn on the shores of our lake, I was coasting in my canoe along one of the islands when I came upon a beautiful little cove. There in center stage was the Wood Duck, a scene I had always wanted to capture.

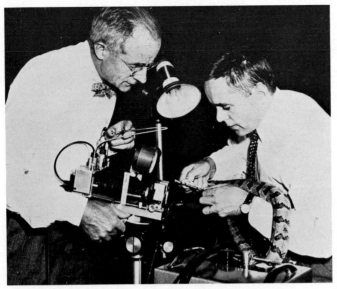

*Author and Norman Harris making picture of venom dropping from fangs of rattlesnake using **Donaldson's Strobe Stereo Camera.***

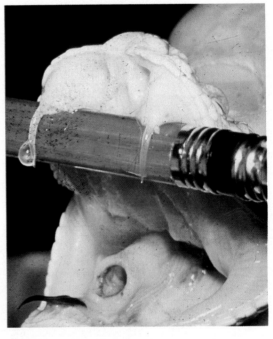

Rattlesnake's open jaws with venom oozing from its fangs. Rattlesnakes are predators of small animals as well as of birds and their eggs.

In November of 1955, Dr. David D. Donaldson of the Howe Laboratories of the Harvard Medical School invited me to see if what he had developed for taking close-up pictures of the human eye could be adapted for use in my nature work.

When I visited him in his laboratory, I found a very sophisticated strobe stereo camera. It had no viewfinder. The field of view was defined by the projection of four dots of light on the subject. It was focused by superimposing the images of the filaments of two lamps. It was weird! After showing me how to operate it, he let me take it home to try it out.

I was delighted with it and brought it back with ideas of a couple of refinements to make it more useful for my purposes. When the changes were completed, I brought it in to the Boston Museum of Science, where Norman D. Harris and I were collaborating on a booklet to be titled *The Eyes of Nature.*

Our first subject from the Museum aviary was "Horny," a Great Horned Owl. He did not like to be photographed in this manner and so complained.

The Saw-whet Owl was a more docile subject. It even allowed us to take extremely close-up pictures of its eyes. As an added protection for the eyes, most birds have a "third" transparent eyelid that completely covers the eye without cutting off the vision. The photograph was made by the Donaldson stereo strobe camera, which stopped the transparent eyelids in the middle of a blink.

Photographing these two Owls seemed much easier than it really was. The camera had to be on a tripod. Moving the bird and the tripod so that the four light dots encompassed the subject area was a feat in its own right. Then the camera had to be focused. The two lenses were attached to the body by a bellows, mounted on a gear-and-pinion track. By turning a knob, the lenses moved forward and back until the filaments were superimposed within the four dots. These two requirements had to be met simultaneously before depressing the cable release to make the exposure.

Saw-whet is tired of having the flash in its eyes.

Author and Snowy Owl

Sometime prior to starting work on *The Eyes of Nature,* I visited the Massachusetts Audubon Society's Moose Hill Wildlife Sanctuary in Sharon. Although I had cameras with me, I was not expecting to take any pictures. I was looking for what I might like to have in my collection. In a remote corner of the spacious display room there was a real live Snowy Owl sitting on its perch twisting its head this way and that. The Snowy Owl is a bird of the far, far north and is rarely seen in New England except occasionally in such locations as northern New Hampshire.

I completed my notes on what I might do later on and put on my hat and heavy overcoat. I was prepared to step out into the cold winter weather when I heard a *whooosh* behind me and felt something drop on my head. Then I heard the director yell, "Blake, stand still, open your camera and point it up towards your head." There was a blinding flash, and I saw him with a camera pointed at me. I was flabbergasted when I saw the results of this perpetration appear in the Boston *Globe* headed "Watch the Birdie."

Sanibel, Florida

In the late 1950s my business life became more demanding, and I was forced to cut drastically the time I spent in the field and in my darkroom. The sale of my sets of stereoscopic bird slides continued, but the whole interest in stereo dwindled. I used to give stereo slide shows, but that did not last very long. It was also complicated. It involved a special projector, a metallic screen and cardboard glasses for the audience. It was not very satisfactory, and I soon gave it up.

In the late 1960s, because of my health, it seemed best to leave New England and move to a warmer climate. I gradually disposed of all my photographic equipment except for my Nikon and Hasselblad. In 1969, we moved into a house we had built on the southwest coast of Florida. As soon as we were settled in I started to look for new bird subjects.

My first subject was the Burrowing Owl. I discovered them among grasses in a depression of a sand dune well above the high water mark. They stared at me as I advanced slowly to take a picture. They seemed quite tame. Although they were much smaller, they reminded me of the Owls I had worked with up north.

These Florida birds dig the burrows by themselves. The nest cavity may be from six inches to three feet in depth. The birds generally stand at the entrance of their nest beside the pile of sand made from the excavation. In the case of an intruder, the Owl may fly off a little way to draw him from the vicinity of the burrow.

One day, a few years later, some friends invited me to go to a prairie-like area where there were a number of scattered nests with birds guarding the entrance of their burrows. Alexander Sprunt, in his *Florida Bird Life,* describes them as follows: "Upper parts are drab, with large white spots on back and wings; underparts are white, heavily blotched with snuff brown."

Pair of Burrowing Owls guard the entrance to their nesting hole.

Burrowing Owl beside nesting hole in a sand dune.

Burrowing Owls in a field.

One of many locations where the Little Blue Heron can be found is in the great cypress swamp called Corkscrew Swamp Sanctuary. This vast area is managed and guarded by the National Audubon Society. As you stroll along the elevated boardwalk and look down at the floating water lettuce, then crane your neck to look up to the top of the towering 300-to-600-year-old trees, you cannot help but feel the awesome spell of the place. There is a mystical silence broken only by the cackling of the Wood Storks feeding their young in nests terraced in the tops of the ancient cypress trees.

The Little Blue Heron is seen here stretching its neck to find some food under the lettuce leaves. The bird is pictured in its mature stage. Previously it was white with blue splotches, and before this it was pure white. Then the young heron, except for its yellow feet, could be mistaken for a Snowy Egret.

Corkscrew scene.

Little Blue Heron in immature stage.

Mature Little Blue Heron.

The Wood Stork is high up on the list of endangered species. It can nest in the Sanctuary only when the water is at the correct level for feeding the wading birds. Some seasons the water is so low that there is a scarcity of food; other times the water may be so high that it is way above wading depth. These fluctuations are in part brought on by the extensive environmental problems that Florida faces.

In spite of all this, the Sanctuary is a treasure house for nature enthusiasts and naturalists alike. There are many kinds of aquatic creatures as well as birds and other animals, and the environment hosts a wide variety of sub-tropical plants and flowers. You can visit the Sanctuary time and time again and always see something new.

Wood Stork alights on upper branch of a cypress tree.

Tiered nests of Wood Storks in a tall cypress tree.

Wood Stork.

Where in Jungle Gardens in Sarasota the more exotic Pink Flamingoes may be found, you may also see mixed in with them an occasional wild Wood Stork or Sandhill Crane.

Flamingoes and a Sandhill Crane.

Jungle Gardens Flamingoes.

Sandhill Cranes feeding.

The Sandhill Cranes are gradually being forced from their natural habitat of the prairies to pastures and even golf courses. They are larger than a Great Blue Heron and appear just as stately. Seen here is a pair feeding. Another view shows the courting dance. The third illustration shows them flying off in tandem, making loud honking noises all the time.

These birds I photographed in a pasture not far from my home. I was separated from them by a wire fence, but they were not far from it and did not seem to object to my presence. Their mating dance was something to behold. I can do nothing better than quote from Forbush to describe it: "The pair danced about, skipping high in the air and even flying up a little way from the ground occasionally turning about, moving with high prancing steps and bowing repeatedly in all directions. Both male and female engage in the dance. Sometimes, even a lone bird may take a few dance steps from time to time." This is exactly what I observed while taking my pictures.

Mating dance of a Sandhill Crane.

Sandhill Cranes flying away in tandem, honking as they go.

I found the Black Skimmers on a sandbar not far from our home. These were standing on the bar sleeping with their heads turned and resting on their backs, while one stayed alert, watching out for predators. Another view shows a bird flying along with its lower mandible under water, scooping up whatever small fish may be in its path. The third shot shows the Skimmers in flight with a couple of Royal Terns that joined the group.

Nuttall wrote in 1833, "The Cut-Water or Black Skimmer appears in New Jersey from its tropical winter quarters early in May. Here it resides and breeds along low sand-bars in the immediate vicinity of the ocean. As the birds remain gregarious through the breeding season it is possible to collect a half bushel or more eggs from a single sand-bar, within the compass of half an acre."

He goes on to say that though the eggs are not very palatable, they are eaten by the inhabitants. The Skimmer's eggs are only about ¼ to ½ inch shorter than those of a hen. I have not checked with my New Jersey friends to see if they are still eating Skimmer eggs. All I know is the birds are here in Florida in the winter where they can be seen and enjoyed.

Black Skimmers sunning, while one keeps watch.

Black Skimmer skimming, scooping up whatever morsels are in its path.

Black Skimmers in flight with a few Royal Terns mixed in.

One of the sanctuaries of the Roseate Spoonbill is in Southwest Florida. I found them in 1980 at the Ding Darling Sanctuary on Sanibel Island.

Like the Pelicans, they nest well up in the mangroves. To feed, they alight on the shore of a shallow estuary or bay. They then wade in and thrust their bills into the water, sometimes even immersing their heads. They move their wide mandibles to and fro, entrapping small fish, crustaceans or insects. Then they proceed to swallow their catch.

These birds are very timid. The only way I was able to obtain satisfactory pictures was to park my car alongside a road that bordered the water and photograph them through a long lens. The Spoonbill is among those other wading birds such as Herons, Egrets and Ibis that suffered the depredation of man in the latter part of the nineteenth century. They were all shot by the hundreds. Their feathers were sold to the millinery trade, where they were used to adorn the hats of ladies of the era. I can remember seeing those elegant headpieces resplendent with brilliant feathers and sometimes even with the head of a bird in front. I often wondered if in a brisk breeze the thing might rise up from the owner's head and take off into the wild blue yonder. As a matter of fact, this never happened because if it was windy, in order not to get the feathers ruffled, the hat was covered by a veil tied firmly under the chin.

The Spoonbill was not used for this purpose as much as the others, but its whole wing was sometimes sold to be used as a fan. These birds were not only destroyed for decoration but sometimes they appeared on the dinner table as delectable squabs.

Shortly after laws were passed protecting birds facing extinction, they began to multiply. In Florida the birds are now facing trouble again due to questionable land use practices and water management policies. However, thanks to the constant vigilance of the National Audubon Society and other dedicated environmental organizations, as well as the State of Florida, the habitats of birds may now be saved and even increased. In the process, more potable water sources may be established.

Spoonbills perching in trees.

Spoonbills under mangroves.

Spoonbills feeding.

Spoonbill with a Louisiana Heron.

Laughing Gulls on the lawn.

The Laughing Gull often basks in the sun on our lawn. Then they stir themselves to do some fishing in the little bay in front of our house. When they return they sometimes go through some courting routines, which we can observe from our kitchen window. Eventually they will all fly off as one. Which bird gives the order for this exodus, I have never been able to figure out. However, they arrive on an island to the south, where they build their nests and raise their young.

117. *Spoonbill swishing bill sideways to filter food before swallowing.*

119. *Laughing gulls on bollards.*

121. *Laughing gulls flying off to nesting site.*

Laughing Gulls hovering over nesting area.

Laughing Gulls sitting on eggs.

Great Blue Herons have become a part of our little community in Englewood, Florida, where we now live. Our Herons have turned into people watchers. They do not walk around with people books tucked under their wings and people glasses hanging from the base of their long necks, but they do cruise around to see what is going on. Occasionally, and sometimes daily, while we are eating lunch on our porch a Heron will walk along very slowly close to the house, peering over the window sills into the room. Its head sways back and forth in rhythm with its legs. Finally, it reaches the sliding glass door. There it stands stock still two arm lengths away, eyeing us and our food. Whether to toss something out or not is a moot question. Authorities say that giving scraps of food and parts of fish will not alter the bird's feeding habits in the wild. It all boils down to a matter of prudence. A false move on the part of a donor may be mistaken as a move of aggression and incite a violent attack. I remember hearing of a similar situation where a Heron thrust its bill right through the blade of a paddle.

Everything is peaceful until the eggs are hatched. As food is provided around the clock, the cackling of the young ones and the croaking of the parents make a disturbing combination of loud, discordant sounds. These can be heard within a radius of half a mile.

All this poses problems. The birds seem to have magically adapted themselves to living and raising their young within the precincts of man. Can man reconcile himself to the sounds and unsanitary habits of a heronry, even if it be made up of only two to three pairs of birds? The encroachment of developments is driving birds, beasts and fish from their natural habitats to either extinction or to unnatural living places.

Is not that the main issue today? It is not only of man and wildlife accommodating themselves to each other, it is men learning to adapt themselves to men of other colors, other philosophies and other climates. Great strides are being made in this direction. Let us help keep them moving.

124. At the top of a tall pine tree, a
125. Heron feeds its young while its
mate supervises the process.

Great Blue Heron at our door.

Great Blue Heron streaking for home.

Heron approaching vicinity of nest.

Epilogue

Of all the states represented in BIRD MAGIC, the birds of Florida are in their most critical habitat. Florida faces the multifaceted problems of destruction of the environment due to unprecedented and impossible growth. Our wetlands and other natural environmental recharge areas are being gobbled up at a phenomenal pace.

The Florida Legislature has finally realized the necessity to do something to preserve and protect our environment. As simple as it seems, it is still an uphill road to convince people in political prominence that the thing that makes Florida attractive is that which we would destroy with our careless attitudes of development. Wading birds are in particular jeopardy. Because of our dredge and fill mentality to create valuable waterfront property and homesites, huge amounts of habitat were destroyed in a wholesale fashion. Over the last four or five years we have restricted, by legislation, this type of activity. Two years ago the Florida Legislature turned its attention to the wetlands. It conferred upon the Department of Environmental Regulations, a state agency, the ability to preserve wetlands in the inland part of the state. This hopefully will secure habitats for wading birds.

The state Governor, Bob Graham, has created as one of his priorities the preservation and restoration of the Everglades, a huge tract in south Florida which serves as a water recharge area and natural habitat for a tremendous variety of flora and fauna, many of which are unique to Florida. Marjory Stoneman Douglas in her famous book, RIVER OF GRASS, demonstrated the importance of preservation of the Everglades. Unfortunately it has taken state government twenty years to realize its import.

Many strides are being made legislatively to protect and preserve our natural habitats. There are now two rivers in Florida which will be designated "Wild and Scenic": the Loxahatchee in central Florida and the Myakka in south Florida for which the designation is currently being sought. The Myakka river is home to many wading birds as well as the endangered Florida panther.

Florida is a unique state and has the opportunity to preserve for all posterity many endangered species — not only the birds depicted herein but the panther and the manatee. Only now are we starting to realize the absolute essential priority we must place on protecting these animals. It has taken many years of hard work to convince the legislature of the rather simple dictum that senseless slaughter is totally unnecessary and an unacceptable approach to life or development.

The conscious considered decision to destroy a species for "progress" may or may not be something that philosophically one can support. However, as a personal note, I cannot. I feel that all life has value but I can intellectually understand — not emotionally accept — a conscious decision to wipe out an entire species out of "necessity.."

I feel that we have convinced most of my colleagues in the Legislature of the necessity to stop creating situations that result in senseless slaughter, and that by altering the way we do some things — not stopping them, but simply altering them — we can protect and preserve not only the wading birds but the rest of Florida's environment.

David L. Thomas, M.D.
Member 1985 Florida Legislature
May 1985